Colonial Williamsburg Cookbook

© Copyright 2019. Laura Sommers.
All rights reserved.
No part of this book may be reproduced in any form or by any electronic or mechanical means without written permission of the author. All text, illustrations and design are the exclusive property of
Laura Sommers

Introduction	1
Williamsburg Cookies	2
Williamsburg Pork Cake	3
Williamsburg Orange Cake	5
Williamsburg Butter Frosting	6
Williamsburg Chicken	7
Colonial Williamsburg Coleslaw	9
Williamsburg Trifle	10
Williamsburg Watermelon Pickle	11
Williamsburg Stew	12
Colonial Williamsburg Cream Of Peanut Soup	13
Williamsburg Scalloped Tomatoes and Artichoke Hearts	14
Williamsburg Bread	15
Williamsburg Casserole	16
Williamsburg Apple Pie	17
Williamsburg Carrot Pudding	19
Williamsburg Breast Of Turkey	21
Williamsburg Chocolate Fudge Cake	22
Williamsburg Sweet Potatoes	23
Williamsburg Bisque Of Hampton Crab	24
Williamsburg Corn Chowder	25

✓ **Williamsburg Golden Gingerbread** 26
✓ **Williamsburg Fruit Punch** 27
✓ **Williamsburg House Aroma** 28
✓ **Williamsburg English Wassail** 29
✓ **Williamsburg Inn Turkey Soup** 30
   Williamsburg Inn Pecan Bars 31
   Williamsburg Pork 33
   Williamsburg Pumpkin Fritters 34
   Williamsburg Orange Sherry Cake 35
   Williamsburg Strawberry Mousse 37
   Williamsburg Sally Lunn 39
   Williamsburg Rice Pudding 40
✓ **Williamsburg Sweet Potatoes** 41
✓ **Williamsburg Sweet Potato Muffins** 42
✓ **Williamsburg Roast Chicken In Brandy** 43
✓ **Williamsburg Wassail Punch** 44
✓ **Williamsburg Sweet Potatoes** 45
✓ **Williamsburg Turkey Soup** 46
   Williamsburg Peas 47
✓ **Williamsburg Brew** 48
✓ **Williamsburg Clam Chowder** 49
   Williamsburg Chicken Surprise 50
   Williamsburg Carrot Cake 51
✓ **Williamsburg Blueberry Muffins** 52

Williamsburg Omelet 53
Williamsburg Potpourri 54
Williamsburg Rice 55
Williamsburg Shortbread 56
Williamsburg Eggnog 57
Williamsburg Pumpkin Soup 58
Williamsburg Hot Tea 59
Williamsburg Frosted Fruit Schrub Drink 60
Williamsburg Sugar Cookie 61
Williamsburg Fish Muddle 62
Williamsburg Gazpacho 64
Williamsburg Apple Dumplings 65
Williamsburg Shepherd's Pie 67
Williamsburg Collops of Salmon 69
Williamsburg Veal Chop 71
Williamsburg Bourbon Balls 72
Williamsburg Creamed Celery with Pecans 73
Colonial Williamsburg Pumpkin Gnocchi 74
Colonial Williamsburg Welsh Rabbit 75
Colonial Williamsburg Tidewater Chili 76
Colonial Williamsburg Chilled Cream of Asparagus Soup 77
Williamsburg Chicken Stock 78
Williamsburg Avocados Stuffed with Crabmeat Rémoulade 79

Rémoulade Sauce	80
Williamsburg Mayonnaise	81
Colonial Williamsburg Caramel Custard	82
Colonial Williamsburg Caramel Syrup	83
About the Author	84
Other Books by Laura Sommers	85

Introduction

Colonial Williamsburg is a historic city in the Commonwealth of Virginia in the United States of America. It is a living museum in that the town and businesses all represent America during the 18th century Colonial period. There are over forty sites and trades to visit including historic taverns, art museums and shops.

When you visit Colonial Williamsburg, you step back in time to the Revolutionary period. You will see how life was for the colonists through shows and reenactments.

This cookbook presents some of the delicious recipes that you will find when you visit Colonial Williamsburg, Virginia as well as other historical recipes from the colonial era.

Williamsburg Cookies

Ingredients:

2 egg whites
2 cups light brown sugar
2 cups chopped pecans
2 tbsps. all-purpose flour
1/2 tsp. salt
1 tsp. vanilla extract
1/2 tbsp. ground cinnamon

Directions:

1. Beat egg whites until stiff.
2. Add salt and beat.
3. Add brown sugar gradually.
4. Sprinkle flour over pecans and add to mixture.
5. Add vanilla.
6. Drop by tsp. onto greased cookie sheet.
7. Bake at 275 degrees F (135 degrees C) for 12 - 15 minutes.

Williamsburg Pork Cake

Ingredients:

1/2 cup brandy
2 1/2 cups raisins
1 1/2 cups dried currants.
1/2 lb. finely ground salt pork
1 cup boiling water
1 cup molasses.
1/2 cup brown sugar
3 1/2 cups all-purpose flour
1 tsp. baking powder
1 tbsp. ground allspice
1 tbsp. ground cinnamon.
1/2 tsp. ground nutmeg.
1/2 tsp. ground cloves

Directions:

1. In a medium saucepan, combine brandy, raisins and currants.
2. Bring to an boil, then remove from heat.
3. Set aside until all liquid is absorbed and mixture is cooled.
4. Preheat oven to 275 degrees F (135 degrees C).
5. Grease and flour a 10 inch tube pan.
6. Sift together the flour, baking powder, allspice, cinnamon, nutmeg and cloves.
7. Set aside.
8. In a large bowl, combine the ground salt pork, boiling water, molasses and sugar.
9. Beat well.
10. Add the flour mixture and beat until incorporated.
11. Stir in the raisin mixture.
12. Pour batter into prepared pan.

13. Bake in the preheated oven for 90 minutes, or until a toothpick inserted into the center of the cake comes out clean.
14. Allow to cool 15 minutes in the pan.
15. Remove from pan and cool completely.

Williamsburg Orange Cake

Ingredients:

2 3/4 cups cake flour
1 1/2 cups white sugar
1 1/2 tsps. baking soda
3/4 tsp. salt.
1/2 cup butter, softened.
1/4 cup shortening
1 1/2 cups buttermilk
3 eggs
1 cup golden raisins, chopped.
1/2 cup chopped walnuts
1 tbsp. orange zest
1 1/2 tsps. vanilla extract
Williamsburg Butter Frosting (see recipe)

Directions:

1. Preheat oven to 350 degrees F (175 degrees C).
2. Grease and flour a 9x13 inch pan, two 9-inch round cake pans, or three 8-inch round cake pans.
3. In a large bowl, combine cake flour, sugar, baking soda and salt.
4. Mix in butter, shortening, buttermilk, eggs, raisins, nuts, orange zest and vanilla.
5. Beat with an electric mixer for 3 minutes on high speed.
6. Pour batter into prepared pan.
7. Bake in preheated oven until a toothpick inserted in center of cake comes out clean.
8. Bake 9x13 inch pan 45 to 50 minutes, or layers 30 to 35 minutes.
9. Allow to cool, and frost with Williamsburg Butter Frosting.

Williamsburg Butter Frosting

Ingredients:

1/2 cup butter, softened
12 tsps. orange liqueur
1 tbsp. orange zest
4 1/2 cups confectioners' sugar

Directions:

1. In a large bowl, blend butter with confectioners' sugar.
2. Stir in orange liqueur and orange zest.
3. Beat until light and fluffy.
4. Use to frost cooled Williamsburg cake.

Williamsburg Chicken

Ingredients:

4 cup Granny Smith apples, diced
1 cup walnuts
1/2 lb. butter
1/2 cup brown sugar
1/2 cup honey
1/2 cup maple syrup
1/4 cup raisins
2 tbsp. nutmeg
4 cup dried bread crumbs
4 chicken breasts (halves)

Raisin Sauce Ingredients:

1/2 cup brown sugar
1/2 cup orange juice
1/2 cup red wine
1/2 cup black current jelly
2 cup chicken stock
1/4 cup raisins
1/4 cup red wine vinegar

Directions:

1. Combine all ingredients except bread crumbs and chicken in saucepan.
2. Cook over medium heat until apples are soft.
3. Remove from heat and let cool.
4. Then add bread crumbs.
5. Pound out chicken breasts, put stuffing in center and roll.
6. Bake at 350 degrees for 1/2 hour.
7. Heap extra stuffing on top.
8. Serve with raisin sauce.

Sauce Directions:

1. Cook all over medium heat until reduced by half, then thicken with flour/butter flour or cornstarch and water.
2. Pour on chicken and serve.

Colonial Williamsburg Coleslaw

Dressing Ingredients:

1 cup cider vinegar
1 cup oil
1 tbsp. salt
2 tsp. sugar
1 tsp. white pepper
2 tsp. celery seeds

Coleslaw Ingredients:

3 lbs. cabbage, shredded
1/2 cup chopped onion
1/4 cup chopped celery
1/4 diced sweet red pepper
Dressing

Dressing Directions:

1. Combine vinegar, oil, salt, sugar, pepper and celery seeds.

Coleslaw Directions:

1. Combine cabbage, onion, celery and red pepper in a bowl.
2. Add dressing and toss.
3. Chill several hours to blend flavors.

Williamsburg Trifle

Ingredients:

1 box yellow cake mix
2 lg. boxes vanilla pudding & pie filling (not instant)
2 (6-10 oz.) boxes frozen strawberries
Whipped topping
Sliced bananas

Directions:

1. Prepare cake according to directions on box.
2. Cool.
3. Prepare pudding according to directions on box.
4. Cool.
5. Thaw strawberries.
6. Assemble approximately 4 hours before serving.
7. Break cake into bite size pieces.
8. Place half of cake in deep dish.
9. Cover with 1 box strawberries.
10. Cover with half of the pudding.
11. Repeat layers.
12. Cover and chill.
13. Just before serving, top with dollops of whipped toppings and sprinkle with almonds.

Williamsburg Watermelon Pickle

Ingredients:

5 lbs. watermelon rind
3 1/2 lbs. sugar
1 pt. water
2 sm. bottles of maraschino cherries
3 sticks cinnamon, broken
2 tbsp. whole cloves
2 tbsp. alum
1 1/2 pts. vinegar

Directions:

1. Peel and cut rind into small pieces and soak in cold water overnight.
2. Drain. Scald in hot water in which alum has been dissolved.
3. Rinse in cold water.
4. Boil together the vinegar, sugar, 1 pint water and spices for 25 minutes.
5. Add rind which has been drained.
6. Boil for 39 minutes.
7. Allow to stand overnight in an enamel container.
8. Next morning add the cherries and boil for 15 minutes.
9. Seal in hot sterilized jars.

Williamsburg Stew

Ingredients:

1 stewing hen or 2 fryers
2 lg. onions, chopped
2 cup cut okra
4 cup or 2 cans tomatoes
2 cup frozen green lima beans
3 med. potatoes, diced
4 cup corn, cut from cob or 2 cans
3 tsp. salt
1 tbsp. sugar

Directions:

1. Simmer chicken pieces in 3 quarts water if thin stew is wanted or 2 quarts water if thick stew is wanted, for 2 1/4 hours.
2. Cook raw vegetables in broth.
3. Add boned and diced chicken.
4. Best cooked long and slow.

Colonial Williamsburg Cream Of Peanut Soup

Ingredients:

1/2 cup butter
1 cup chopped celery
1 cup chopped onion
1-1 1/2 cup creamy style peanut butter
1 cup light cream
2-3 tbsp. flour
2 qt. chicken broth
Chopped peanuts

Directions:

1. Puree celery and onions then sauté in butter.
2. Add flour until blended in thoroughly.
3. Stir in chicken broth and bring to boil.
4. Add peanut butter and simmer about 20 minutes until peanut butter is dissolved.
5. Should be brownish in color and slightly thick.
6. Add cream and stir. Serve with chopped peanuts on top.

Williamsburg Scalloped Tomatoes and Artichoke Hearts

Ingredients:

1 can (2 lbs.) whole tomatoes
1 can (14 oz.) artichoke hearts
1 sm. onion, chopped
4 tbsp. butter
1/2 tsp. basil
1 tsp. sugar
Salt and pepper to taste

Directions:

1. Preheat oven to 325 degrees.
2. Grease shallow casserole dish.
3. Drain tomatoes and artichokes; rinse and quarter artichokes.
4. Sauté onions in butter until tender.
5. Add tomatoes, artichokes, basil; heat 2 or 3 minutes, stirring gently.
6. Season with sugar, salt and pepper.
7. Bake at 325 degrees for 10 to 15 minutes or until vegetables are heated through.

Williamsburg Bread

Ingredients:

2 pkg. crescent rolls
2 (8 oz.) pkg. cream cheese
1 cup sugar
1 egg yolks (reserve white)
1 tsp. vanilla

Topping Ingredients:

1/2 cup sugar
2 tsp. cinnamon
1 sm. pkg. pecans

Directions:

1. Spread 1 package of crescent rolls on bottom of greased 9 x 13 inch pan.
2. Mix cream cheese, 1 cup sugar, egg yolk and vanilla.
3. Spread over layer of crescent rolls. Put second package of crescent rolls on top.
4. Brush with egg white and sprinkle on top.
5. Bake at 350 degrees for 30-35 minutes.

Williamsburg Casserole

Ingredients:

5 cup Rice Krispies
2 cup long rice
1 can milk (evaporated)
1 can cream of mushroom soup
1 chopped med. onion
12 oz. grated sharp cheese
2 lb. ball sausage

Directions:

1. Grease 9 x 12 inch covered casserole.
2. Pour Rice Krispies in evenly.
3. Brown sausage and onions (sautéed); drain well.
4. Cook rice 5 minutes.
5. Drain.
6. Add mushroom soup and milk.
7. Stir and remove from heat.
8. Crumble sausage and onion over Rice Krispies then add the rice mixture. Put cheese on top.
9. Bake 1 hour in 350 degree oven.

Williamsburg Apple Pie

Ingredients:

2 cup un-sifted flour
1 tsp. salt
2/3 cup stick butter
6-7 tbsp. ice water
1/2 cup apricot preserves
1 tbsp. lemon juice
1 tsp. grated lemon peel
7 cup diced, pared baking apples
1/2 cup sugar
3 tbsp. flour
1/4 tsp. ground cinnamon
1/4 tsp. ground nutmeg
2 tbsp. stick butter

Directions:

1. Measure 2 cups flour and salt into a bowl.
2. Cut in 2/3 cup butter with pastry blender or 2 knives until mixture resembles coarse meal.
3. Gradually sprinkle in ice water, stirring well after each addition.
4. On lightly floured board, roll out 1/2 of dough to fit a 9" pie plate.
5. Transfer to plate and trim extra edge leaving 1/2" over hanging.
6. In a bowl, combine preserves, lemon juice and peel.
7. Mix in apples.
8. Combine sugar, remaining 3 tbsps. flour, cinnamon and nutmeg.
9. Sprinkle over apple mixture; toss well.
10. Pile into pie plate; dot with remaining 2 tbsps. butter.
11. Roll out remaining pastry for top crust; make slits for steam to escape during baking.
12. Place over filling; seal and finish edges.

13. If glaze is desired, brush pastry with beaten egg.
14. Bake at 400 degrees F for 55 to 60 minutes or until done.

Williamsburg Carrot Pudding

Ingredients:

3 eggs, separated
4 tbsp. sugar
1 1/2 tbsp. cornstarch
1 cup milk
3 cup (2 lb.) carrots, cooked and mashed
3 tbsp. butter
1 tsp. salt
1 cup fine bread crumbs
1 cup light cream
1/2 tsp. fresh grated nutmeg
1/4 cup cream sherry

Directions:

1. Preheat the oven to 300 degrees.
2. Grease a 2-quart casserole.
3. Beat the egg yolks and sugar until they are light and fluffy; hold.
4. Mix the cornstarch with a small amount of milk.
5. Heat the remaining milk, add the cornstarch, and stir until the mixture is smooth and slightly thickened.
6. Stir a small amount of the hot cornstarch mixture into the egg yolks and sugar.
7. Stir to mix well, then pour the yolks mixture into the hot milk and cornstarch.
8. Cook, stirring, over medium heat until the mixture is smooth and thick.
9. Add the carrots, butter, salt, and bread crumbs.
10. Blend evenly.
11. Stir in the cream and add the nutmeg and sherry.
12. Mix well.
13. Beat the egg whites until they hold firm peaks.
14. Fold them into the carrot mixture.
15. Pour into the prepared casserole.

16. Place the casserole in a pan of hot water and bake at 300 degrees for 30 minutes.
17. Increase the heat to 350 degrees and bake for an additional 45 minutes or until a knife inserted in the center comes out clean.

Williamsburg Breast Of Turkey

Ingredients:

1/2 cup butter
1/2 cup all-purpose flour
2 cup hot chicken stock or canned chicken broth
1 tsp. salt
1/8 tsp. white pepper
1 cup milk
1 cup light cream
1 lb. turkey breast, sliced
Cooked rice or noodles
3 tbsp. toasted almonds, chopped

Directions:

1. Melt the butter and add the flour, stirring until smooth.
2. Pour the hot chicken stock into the butter-flour mixture and stir until smooth.
3. Add the salt and pepper.
4. Heat the milk and cream in a saucepan.
5. Pour into the thickened chicken stock and cook over low heat for 10 minutes, stirring often.
6. Serve the sauce very hot over sliced turkey breast and steamed noodles or rice.
7. Top with the toasted almonds.

Williamsburg Chocolate Fudge Cake

Ingredients:

1 cup butter
2 cup sugar
4 eggs
2 cup sifted flour
1/4 tsp. salt
1 1/2 tsp. baking soda
2/3 cup buttermilk
1 tsp. vanilla
3 oz. unsweetened chocolate, grated

Directions:

1. Preheat oven to 325 degrees.
2. Grease and flour two 9 inch round 1 1/2 inch pans.
3. Cream butter and sugar.
4. Add the eggs one at a time and beat well after each addition.
5. After the last egg has been added, beat for 1 minute or until the mixture is light and fluffy. Sift the flour with the salt.
6. Mix the baking soda with the buttermilk and add alternately with the flour to the creamed mixture.
7. Add the vanilla.
8. Melt the chocolate in 2/3 cup of boiling water.
9. Stir until smooth. Blend the chocolate into the cake mixture.
10. Pour into the prepared pan and bake for 45 minutes to 1 hour at 325 degrees or until the cake tests done.
11. Cool in the pan.
12. Frost with Chocolate Fudge Frosting.

Williamsburg Sweet Potatoes

Ingredients:

3 lb. sweet potatoes
3/4 cup light brown sugar, packed
3 tbsp. butter
1/2 tsp. cinnamon
1/4 tsp. salt
1 cup milk
1/2 tsp. nutmeg

Directions:

1. Grease 1 1/2 quart casserole.
2. Cook potatoes in boiling salted water until done.
3. Peel and mash.
4. Stir in all remaining ingredients except 2 tbsps. of sugar.
5. Turn mixture into prepared casserole and sprinkle with remaining sugar.
6. Bake for 30 minutes in 400 degree oven.

Williamsburg Bisque Of Hampton Crab

Ingredients:

1 cup crabmeat
1 can cream of mushroom soup
1 can cream of asparagus soup
1 cup light cream
1 1/4 cup milk
1 tsp. Worcestershire sauce
1/2 cup dry sherry
Dash of Tabasco

Directions:

1. Blend all ingredients in blender.
2. Heat but do not boil. Serves 8.

Williamsburg Corn Chowder

Ingredients:

3 oz. salt pork, cubed, or bacon
1 lg. onion, chopped
1 rib celery, chopped
1 1/2 cup potatoes, diced
2 cup chicken stock or canned chicken or cream of chicken soup
2 cup cream style corn
2 cup milk
1/4 cup butter
Salt and pepper to taste

Directions:

1. Fry bacon or pork until brown, add the onion and saute over medium heat 5 minutes, stirring often.
2. Add celery, potatoes, chicken stock, and 1 cup of water, and simmer until potatoes are done.
3. Add corn and simmer 5 minutes, stirring occasionally.
4. Heat the milk and butter.
5. Add to the soup.
6. Add salt and pepper to taste.

Williamsburg Golden Gingerbread

Ingredients:

1 stick butter
1/2 cup white sugar
1 cup honey
3 eggs
3 cup flour
2 tbsp. ginger
1 tsp. ground coriander
1 tsp. mace
1 tsp. cinnamon
1 tsp. cream of tartar
1 tsp. soda
1/2 cup warm sweet milk
3 tbsp. orange juice
1 tsp. orange extract

Directions:

1. Cream butter and sugar.
2. Stir in honey.
3. Mix well, and add eggs, continuing to mix.
4. Slowly stir in flour and spices.
5. Dissolve cream of tartar and soda in milk, and stir into the batter.
6. Add juice and extract.
7. Mix well, and spoon into greased miniature muffin tins.
8. Bake at 325 degrees for about 20 minutes.
9. Makes 4 to 5 dozen.

Williamsburg Fruit Punch

Ingredients:

1 qt. strong tea
1 cup lemon juice
2 cup orange juice
1 cup sugar
3/4 qt. cranberry or grape juice
1 qt. water
1 pt. ginger ale

Directions:

1. Make tea from 4 tea bags or 6 tsps. instant tea.
2. Mix tea, fruit juices, sugar and chill.
3. Just before serving, add ginger ale.
4. Pour ice cubes in punch bowl.

Williamsburg House Aroma

Ingredients:

3/4 tsp. ground cloves
3/4 tsp. ground cinnamon
Heaping tsp. instant orange peel
1 tsp. whole cloves
Several twists fresh orange peel
2 cup cold water

Directions:

1. Mix together all ingredients.
2. Pour into pint Mason jars and decorate with calico and ribbon if using for holiday gifts.
3. Simmer on stove in small saucepan.
4. Add more water as necessary.
5. Makes your house smell wonderful for holiday entertaining!

Williamsburg English Wassail

Ingredients:

4 cup sweet apple cider
1 cup orange juice
1/2 cup lemon juice
1 1/2 cup pineapple juice

Directions:

1. Place the following in a coffee pot basket: 1 tsp. whole cloves 4 tbsp. brown sugar
2. When the pot stops perking, it's ready!

Williamsburg Inn Turkey Soup

Ingredients:

1 turkey carcass
4 qts. water
3 lg. onions, chopped
3 stalks celery, chopped
2 lg. carrots, chopped
1/2 tsp. poultry seasoning, if desired
1/4 cup uncooked rice
1 cup butter
1 1/2 cup flour
1 pt. half & half
3 cup diced & cooked turkey
Salt & pepper

Directions:

1. In large kettle, cook turkey carcass with water to make 3 quarts stock.
2. Remove bones, reserve meat for soup, strain stock, set aside.
3. In saucepan, combine onions, celery, carrots, rice and 1 quart of the stocks.
4. Cook for 20 minutes, set aside. In large soup kettle, melt butter, blend in flour and heat until bubbly.
5. Add half and half and remaining 2 quarts stock to butter-flour mixture.
6. Cook and stir until bubbly.
7. Stir in reserved vegetable mixture, turkey, seasoning.
8. Heat slowly to serving temperature. This soup freezes well.

Williamsburg Inn Pecan Bars

Ingredients:

1 cup butter
1 cup light brown sugar
1 cup honey
1/2 cup whipping cream
3 cup pecans, chopped

Sugar Dough Ingredients:

3/4 cup butter
3/4 cup sugar
2 eggs
Rind of 1 lemon grated
3 cup sifted all purpose flour
1/2 tsp. baking powder

Directions:

1. Grease and flour two 9 x 9 x 2 inch baking pans.
2. Heat oven to 375 degrees 10 minutes before dough is ready to go into oven.

Dough Directions:

1. Cream butter, sugar add eggs and lemon rind, beat well. Sift flour, baking powder together; add to creamed mixture.
2. Beat well. Chill dough until firm enough to handle. Press dough into bottom and sides of prepared pans. Dough will be approximately 1/8 inch thick. Prick all over with a fork.
3. Bake 12 to 15 minutes at 375 degrees or until dough looks half done.

Filling Directions:

1. Combine butter, sugar and honey in deep saucepan; stir and boil for 5 minutes.
2. Remove; cool slightly; add cream; chopped pecans.
3. Mix well.
4. Spread topping evenly over surface of partially baked sugar dough with buttered wooden spoon or flexible spatula.
5. Bake 30 to 35 minutes at 350 degrees. Cool and cut into 1 x 2 inch bars.

Williamsburg Pork

Ingredients:

4 lg. pork chops or pork filets
1 onion, cut in thick slices
1/4 cup creamy peanut butter (not crunchy)
1/2 can cream of mushroom soup
1/4 cup milk
1 tsp. Worcestershire sauce
1 tsp. salt
1/2 tsp. pepper

Directions:

1. Trim fat from the chops or filets.
2. Brown the meat in a skillet over medium heat. Top each chop with a slice of onion.
3. Mix the remaining ingredients and pour over the chops.
4. Cover skillet and simmer over low heat for 45 minutes until tender. Serve immediately.

Williamsburg Pumpkin Fritters

Ingredients:

1 egg
1/2 cup sugar
1/2 tsp. salt
1 1/2 cup canned pumpkin
1 cup all-purpose flour
1 tsp. baking powder
1/4 tsp. baking soda
2 tsp. pumpkin pie spice
1/2 tsp. ginger
1 tbsp. butter, melted
1 tsp. vanilla
Confectioners' sugar

Directions:

1. Beat the egg, sugar, and salt until very light and fluffy. Blend in the pumpkin. Sift the flour, baking powder, and baking soda together.
2. Beat into the pumpkin mixture.
3. Add the spices, butter, and vanilla.
4. Mix well. Drop by tablespoonfuls onto a well-greased hot griddle or fry in deep hot fat a teaspoonful at a time. Watch carefully - the fritters scorch easily.
5. Sprinkle with confectioners' sugar.

Williamsburg Orange Sherry Cake

Cake Ingredients:

1 cup golden raisins
1/2 cup dry sherry
2 1/2 cup sifted unbleached flour
1 1/2 tsp. baking soda
1/2 tsp. salt
3/4 cup unsalted butter at room temperature
1/2 cup dark brown sugar
1 cup granulated sugar
3 eggs
1 1/2 tsp. vanilla extract
Finely grated zest of 1 orange
1 1/2 cup buttermilk
1/2 cup chopped pecans

Frosting Ingredients:

1/2 cup unsalted butter at room temperature
1 lb. confectioners sugar
4-5 tbsp. Cointreau or other orange liqueur
2 tbsp. finely grated orange zest
Orange slices and pecan halves for garnish

Directions:

1. The night before you plan to make the cake, soak the raisins in the sherry and continue soaking overnight. The following day, preheat oven to 350 degrees. Butter and flour 2 (9-inch) cake pans.
2. To make the cake, sift the flour, baking soda, and salt together and set aside. Cream the butter and sugars in a large mixing bowl.

3. Add the eggs, one at a time, beating well after each addition.
4. Beat in the vanilla and grated orange zest.
5. Add the flour alternately with the buttermilk, beating well after each addition.
6. Stir in the pecans and raisins with sherry.
7. Pour the batter into the prepared pans.
8. Bake until the cake begins to pull away from the edge of the pan and springs back when lightly touched in the center, 35-40 minutes. Let cool 10 minutes. Invert onto wire racks to cool completely.
9. To make the frosting, cream the butter, sugar and enough of the Cointreau to make the frosting spreadable but not runny.
10. Beat in the orange zest.
11. Place 1 cake layer on a serving plate and spread evenly with some of the frosting. Top with the second layer and frost the top and side of the cake. Decorate the top of the cake with orange slices and pecan halves.
12. Makes 12 portions.

Williamsburg Strawberry Mousse

Ingredients:

1 pt. strawberries or 2 pkgs. (10 oz.) frozen strawberries
OMIT SUGAR
2 pkgs. (3 oz. each) strawberry flavor gelatin
1/4 cup sugar
1 pt. whipping cream

Directions:

1. Crush strawberries and drain the juice, reserve it.
2. Add enough water to the juice to make 1 1/2 cups.
3. Bring the juice to a boil and stir in gelatin, dissolve and cool.
4. Add strawberries and sugar.
5. Whip cream until it stands in soft peaks and fold into strawberry mixture.
6. Pour mixture into a 2 quart ring mold.

Williamsburg Salad Dressing

Ingredients:

1/2 cup red wine vinegar
1/4 cup sugar
1/4 cup honey
1 tsp. dry mustard
1 tsp. paprika
1 tsp. celery seed
1 tsp. celery salt
1 cup vegetable oil

Directions:

1. Combine first 5 ingredients in saucepan.
2. Bring to boil for 3 minutes.
3. Remove from heat. Cool.
4. Add celery spices and oil. Shake and serve. Best if cold.

Williamsburg Sally Lunn

Ingredients:

1 pkg. dry yeast
1 cup warm milk
1/2 cup butter
1/3 cup sugar
3 eggs
4 cup flour

Directions:

1. Put yeast in warm water (not over 108 degrees). Cream together 1/2 cup butter and 1/3 cup sugar.
2. Add 3 eggs and beat well.
3. Sift in 4 cups flour alternately with milk and yeast mixture, beating well. Let rise in a warm place, then beat well.
4. Pour into well greased Sally Lunn pan (can use bundt pan) or muffin pans. Let rise again before baking in a moderate oven.

Williamsburg Rice Pudding

Ingredients:

4 eggs
3/4 cup sugar
2 cup milk
1 1/2 cup cooked rice (not instant)
1 1/2 tsp. lemon juice
1 1/2 tsp. vanilla
1/2 tsp. nutmeg
1 tbsp. butter
2/3 cup raisins

Directions:

1. Grease a 2 quart square Pyrex or Corningware dish.
2. Combine eggs, sugar, milk and beat well.
3. Add remaining ingredients, stir well.
4. Pour into pan.
5. Place the dish in a pan of boiling water and bake in oven at 350 degrees for 45 minutes. Custard will come to the top when in oven for 5 minutes.
6. Stir once.

Williamsburg Sweet Potatoes

Ingredients:

1/2 cup butter
1 1/4 cup sugar
2 eggs
1 1/4 cup sweet potato, mashed
1 1/2 cup all purpose flour
2 tsp. baking powder
1/4 tsp. salt
1 tsp. cinnamon
1/4 tsp. nutmeg
1 cup milk
1/4 cup pecans
1/4 cup raisins

Directions:

1. Preheat oven to 400 degrees.
2. Grease muffin pans. Cream butter and sugar.
3. Add eggs, mix well; blend in sweet potatoes. Sift flour, baking powder, salt and spices.
4. Add to other mixture alternately with milk. Do not over mix. Fold in nuts and raisins.
5. Fill tins 1/2 full.
6. Bake 25 minutes. Batter can be made ahead and stored in refrigerator for 3 or 4 days.

Williamsburg Sweet Potato Muffins

Ingredients:

1/2 cup butter
1 1/4 cup sugar
2 eggs
1 1/4 cup sweet potatoes, mashed
1 1/2 cup all-purpose flour
2 tsp. baking powder
1/4 tsp. salt
1 tsp. cinnamon
1/4 tsp. nutmeg
1 cup milk
1/4 cup pecans, chopped
1/4 cup raisins (optional)

Directions:

1. Preheat oven to 400 degrees.
2. Grease muffin pans. Cream butter, sugar, add eggs.
3. Mix well, blend in sweet potatoes. Sift flour, baking powder, salt and spices, and add to first mixture alternately with milk. Don't over mix. Fold in nuts and raisins.
4. Fill tins half full and bake 25 minutes.

Williamsburg Roast Chicken In Brandy

Ingredients:

1 lg. roasting chicken, cut in serving size pieces
Salt to taste
Pepper to taste
3 cup dry white wine
1/2 cup butter
1 cup brandy

Directions:

1. Salt and pepper chicken.
2. Marinate in wine overnight. Saute chicken in butter until golden brown.
3. Place in a roaster with the butter and the marinade.
4. Cover.
5. Bake in preheated 375 degree oven for 50 minutes.
6. Add more wine if necessary while baking. Lower heat to 350 degrees. Roast until tender. When serving, place chicken on warm platter and pour brandy over it. Ignite and bring to the table flaming. Use leftover juices in the plate to quench the flames.

Williamsburg Wassail Punch

Ingredients:

1 gallon apple juice
4 good size apples
3-4 lg. oranges
1 cup raisins
1 oz. rum extract
1/2 cup rum
2 tbsp. allspice
Cinnamon sticks
1 qt. tea
Sugar

Directions:

1. Night before, slice the oranges.
2. Cut apples into quarters.
3. Place raisins into a large bowl, then add the rum extract (small bottle), rum, and allspice. Blend together.
4. Cover; let stand in the refrigerator overnight.
5. Next day, place in crock pot at least 1 hour before serving.
6. Add in the mixture the tea and sugar to taste. Then add the cinnamon sticks. Serve piping hot. Serves 24.

Williamsburg Sweet Potatoes

Ingredients:

2 1/2 lbs. sweet potatoes
1/2 cup butter
2 cup milk
1 tsp. salt
3/4 cup sugar
1/4 tsp. cinnamon
1/2 tsp. nutmeg

Directions:

1. Cook sweet potatoes until tender.
2. Drain off cooking liquid and mash.
3. Beat well sweet potatoes and all remaining ingredients.
4. Pour in greased casserole dish and bake at 400 degrees for 30 minutes or until glazed on top.

Williamsburg Turkey Soup

Ingredients:

1 turkey carcass
4 qt. water
1 cup butter
1 cup all-purpose flour
3 chopped onions
2 lg. carrots, chopped
2 stalks celery, chopped
2 tsp. salt
3/4 tsp. pepper
2 cup half & half
1 cup white rice

Directions:

1. Place turkey carcass and water in large Dutch oven; bring to boil.
2. Cover and reduce heat, and simmer 1 hour.
3. Remove carcass from broth, and pick meat from bones. Set broth and meat aside.
4. Measure broth; add water, if necessary, to measure 3 quarts.
5. Heat butter in large Dutch oven; add flour, and cook over medium heat, stirring constantly 5 minutes. (Roux should be very light in color.) Stir onion, carrot, celery into roux; cook over medium heat 10 minutes; stirring often.
6. Add broth, turkey, rice, salt and pepper; cook 20 minutes or until rice is done.
7. Add half & half, heat through.

Williamsburg Peas

Ingredients:

1 can sweet peas
1 tbsp. peanut butter
1 tbsp. butter
1 tbsp. chopped parsley
Salt & pepper

Directions:

1. Melt butter in a small skillet, add the can of peas, including the juice. Distribute peanut butter over the peas.
2. Add salt and pepper to taste.
3. Toss carefully.
4. Let the peas boil gently until the peanut butter is dissolved.
5. Mix in chopped parsley and serve.

Williamsburg Brew

Ingredients:

1 qt. pineapple juice
1 qt. water
2 tbsp. pickling spice
6 cinnamon sticks
1 qt. apple juice
1 tbsp. allspice
16 whole cloves

Directions:

1. Simmer brew in saucepan on lowest setting on stove.
2. Add water as it cooks down.
3. Enjoy the pleasant aroma throughout your home.

Williamsburg Clam Chowder

Ingredients:

12 lg. clams
1/4 lb. bacon fat or salt pork
2 med. onions, chopped
3 med. potatoes, cubed
Salt and white pepper
2 tbsp. cornmeal or all-purpose flour
1 cup light cream

Directions:

1. Scrub clams and steam in enough water to cover.
2. Remove clams from shells, chop fine, reserve. Strain the liquid; add enough water to make 6 cups.
3. Cut bacon or pork in 1/2 inch cubes. Fry until crisp.
4. Add onions, potatoes, clams and liquid.
5. Simmer until potatoes are done.
6. Add salt and pepper.
7. Mix flour and cornmeal with a little cold water and stir into chowder.
8. Add cream.
9. Scallops can also be added.

Williamsburg Chicken Surprise

Ingredients:

1 chicken boiled
Salt & pepper
2 tbsp. parsley
2 tbsp. onion
2 tbsp. celery
Ham slices
Almonds

Dressing Ingredients:

2 cup bread crumbs
1 minced onion
2 tbsp. parsley
1/2 tsp. sage & savory
Salt & pepper
Moisten with chicken broth
2 cup white sauce

Directions:

1. Boil chicken with parsley, onion, celery salt and pepper. When tender place in casserole dish.
2. Make dressing out of bread and seasonings.
3. Spread ham slices with dressing. Press almonds in center and roll up.
4. Place in casserole with chicken.
5. Cover with white sauce and bake in 350 degree oven for 45 minutes.

Williamsburg Carrot Cake

Ingredients:

4 eggs, well beaten
1 1/2 cup vegetable oil
2 tsp. baking powder
2 tsp. cinnamon
3 cup grated carrots
2 cup sugar
2 tsp. baking soda
2 cup flour
1 tsp. salt
Beat eggs, add the other ingredients, except carrots.
Mix well, then fold in 3 cups grated carrots.
Bake at 350 degrees for 45-50 minutes.
ICING:
1/2 stick butter
8 oz. cream cheese
1/2 tsp. vanilla
16 oz. confectioners sugar

Directions:

1. Beat butter and cream cheese, then add other ingredients until creamy.
2. Make sure cake is cool before icing.

Williamsburg Blueberry Muffins

Ingredients:

1/3 cup vegetable shortening
1 cup sugar
2 eggs
1 3/4 cup all-purpose flour
2 tsp. baking powder
1/2 tsp. salt
2/3 cup milk
1 1/2 cup blueberry (fresh)
1 tbsp. sugar
2 tbsp. all-purpose flour

Directions:

1. Preheat oven to 400 degrees; grease muffin tin. Cream shortening and sugar until light and fluffy.
2. Add eggs, one at a time, beating well after each.
3. Stir flour, baking powder, and salt together.
4. Add the dry ingredients and milk alternately, mixing until just blended. Do not overmix.
5. Add blueberries with the sugar and flour.
6. Add blueberries to batter, folding just enough to mix well.
7. Fill cups 2/3 full. A little sugar and cinnamon may be sprinkled on top.
8. Bake at 400 degrees for 20-25 minutes. If frozen blueberries, toss gently in paper towels to remove ice crystals, but do not thaw. If canned, drain very well.

Williamsburg Omelet

Ingredients:

16 slices bread, buttered and decrusted
1 1/2 cup shredded Cheddar cheese
1 1/2 cup chopped ham
3 cup milk
1 cup cream
7 eggs
1 sm. jar sliced mushrooms

Directions:

1. Butter a 9 x 13 inch pan. Put 8 slices of bread on bottom.
2. Spread cheese; then, ham and mushrooms. Put 8 slices of bread on top - butter side up.
3. Mix milk, cream and eggs; then pour over top ending with 8 slices of bread.

Williamsburg Potpourri

Ingredients:

1 qt. dried flower petals
1 oz. ground cinnamon
1 oz. ground nutmeg
1 oz. ground cloves
1 oz. sliced gingerroot
1/2 oz. anise seed
2 oz. powdered arrowroot
Whole cloves, crushed
Cinnamon sticks, crushed

Directions:

1. Mixed dried petals, ground cinnamon, nutmeg, cloves, gingerroot, anise seed and arrowroot. Store in covered jar. When company comes, place in an attractive bowl or dish. if left uncovered, occasionally add a few crushed cloves and crushed cinnamon sticks to the mixture to restore the fragrance.

Williamsburg Rice

Ingredients:

1 stick butter
1 cup raw rice, rinsed
2 tbsp. fresh parsley or 1 tsp. dried parsley flakes
1 (4 oz.) can mushroom pieces
2 (10 oz.) cans beef consomme
Dash or 2 of seasoning salt

Directions:

1. Melt butter in casserole in oven.
2. Remove and add remaining ingredients.
3. Stir well and bake uncovered in 350 degree oven for 1 hour.

Williamsburg Shortbread

Ingredients:

2 1/2 cup flour
2 sticks butter
1/2 cup sugar

Directions:

1. Press in small jelly roll pan that has been greased.
2. Bake for 1 hour at 275 degrees.
3. Remove and cut in squares while still hot.

Williamsburg Eggnog

Ingredients:

1/4 cup sugar
1/4 tsp. cinnamon
1/4 tsp. ginger
1/4 tsp. ground cloves
6 well beaten eggs
2 qt. orange juice, chilled
1/2 cup lemon juice, chilled
1 qt. vanilla ice cream
1 qt. ginger ale

Directions:

1. Beat sugar and spices into beaten eggs.
2. Stir in chilled orange and lemon juices.
3. Cut ice cream in chunks.
4. Place in punch bowl. Slowly pour gingerale down side of bowl. Gently stir in egg mixture.
5. Sprinkle with nutmeg.
6. Makes about 20 servings.

Williamsburg Pumpkin Soup

Ingredients:

1/4 cup finely chopped onion
4 tbsp. butter
1 can cream of chicken soup or cream of mushroom soup
1 cup canned pumpkin
1/2 tsp. ground nutmeg
1/2 tsp. salt
Dash of pepper
1 soup can water

Directions:

1. In saucepan, cook onions in butter until tender.
2. Stir in soup, pumpkin, and seasonings.
3. Gradually add water.
4. Heat; stir occasionally. Garnish with parsley.
5. Makes 2 1/2 cups.

Williamsburg Hot Tea

Ingredients:

1 qt. water
2 qt. cranberry juice
2 qt. pineapple juice
2 lemons, sliced
1 tbsp. cloves
2 sticks cinnamon

Directions:

1. Use large 30-cup percolator.
2. Mix all liquids.
3. Arrange lemon, cloves and cinnamon on basket.

Williamsburg Frosted Fruit Schrub Drink

Ingredients:

Ice
1 cup apricot juice
1/2 cup grapefruit juice
1 cup pineapple juice
16 oz. lemon ice
Sprig of mint

Directions:

1. Blend the above ingredients in a blender together.

Williamsburg Sugar Cookie

Ingredients:

1/2 cup butter
1 cup sugar
1/2 cup vegetable oil (Mazola or Crisco)
1 egg
1 tsp. vanilla
2 3/4 cup all purpose flour
1/4 tsp. salt
1 tsp. baking soda
1 tsp. cream of tartar

Directions:

1. Cream butter, sugar and vegetable oil; add well beaten egg.
2. Add vanilla, flour, salt, soda and cream of tartar. Drop onto greased baking sheet by teaspoonful. Press with bottom of glass slightly greased and dipped in sugar.
3. Bake at 350 degrees for 8 to 10 minutes, will brown rapidly after 7 minutes in some ovens. Should be lightly browned. Use well greased cookie sheets, cookies are very fragile.

Williamsburg Fish Muddle

Ingredients:

2 lbs. fillets of striped bass, haddock or cod
2 bay leaves
1 large Spanish onion
2 carrots, cubed
2 stalks celery, chopped (with leaves)
1/2 tsp. whole mixed peppercorns
1/4 tsp. Tabasco
Sea salt and cracked black pepper, to taste
1/4 lb. pancetta, cut into 1/8" cubes
6 green onions, finely chopped
1/4 cup fresh parsley
2 cloves garlic, minced
Fresh lemon wedges

Directions:

1. This soup is a cousin to fish chowder, an old traditional dish from the Atlantic Coast. Any type of white fish with few bones may be used.
2. Heat pancetta in 2 tbsps. of water in a Dutch oven; as the water evaporates, add 1 tbsp. olive oil. As the pancetta browns, add green onions, Spanish onion and chopped celery; saute until soft.
3. Add the fish.
4. Add barely enough water to cover the fish.
5. Cover the pot and simmer until the fish is opaque and white and begins to flake.
6. Remove it to a dish using a slotted spoon and set aside.
7. Add 2 cloves minced garlic, and the bay leaves, carrots and peppercorns and half of the parsley.
8. Simmer, uncovered, for 15 minutes.
9. Add the potatoes and cook until tender.

10. Meanwhile, check the poached fish for bones. When the potatoes are tender, return the fish to the broth and simmer for another 10 minutes.
11. Add Tabasco, to taste. Adjust seasoning, adding salt and pepper, if needed.
12. Remove and discard bay leaves.
13. Ladle a large portion of fish into serving bowls, and top with potatoes, then a few spoons of the broth on top. The broth may be strained and boiled for several minutes to reduce the quantity and strengthen the flavor.
14. Add a touch of minced parsley at the top and a sprig of parsley to the side for each serving. Serve with Pilot or chowder crackers and fresh lemon wedges.

Variations: Finely diced lean salt pork may be used instead of the pancetta.
Add sweet corn with the potatoes for another, heartier variation. Some like to add chopped vine-ripened tomatoes to the broth; if tomatoes are used, don't forget fresh basil.

Cooks Note: This is not a chowder and should be served with both a fork and a spoon; the broth shouldn't be thickened with flour, but served as-is.

Williamsburg Gazpacho

Ingredients:

4 cucumbers, peeled, seeded and cut into l-inch slices
1/2 large Spanish or Bermuda onion, peeled and diced
1/2 stalk celery, sliced
1/2 green pepper. seeds and ribs removed, and cut into strips
1 large ripe tomato, peeled and seeded
1 garlic clove, peeled and minced
1¼ cups broken pieces of white bread
2 tbsps. extra virgin olive oil
1 cup water
2 tbsps. red wine vinegar
1/2 tsp. salt, or to taste
2 cups tomato or V8 juice
Freshly ground black pepper to taste

Directions:

1. Pass the cucumbers, onion, celery, green pepper, tomato, garlic and bread through the small die of a meat grinder, or chop finely (but do not puree) in a food processor fitted with the steel blade, using on and off pulsing action.
2. Combine with the remaining ingredients, season to taste and stir well. Serve very chilled.

Williamsburg Apple Dumplings

Pastry Ingredients:

1/4 cup all-vegetable shortening
1 3/4 cups all-purpose flour
1/2 tsp. salt
1/4 pound (1 stick) unsalted butter, chilled
4 to 6 tbsps. ice water

Apples Ingredients:

4 small tart apples, such as Granny Smith
1 tbsp. raisins
1 tbsps. dark rum
4 tsps. unsalted butter

Syrup Ingredients:

1 cup firmly packed dark brown sugar
1 1/2 cups water
2 tbsps. unsalted butter

Directions:

1. To make the pastry, combine the shortening, flour and salt in a food processor fitted with the steel blade. Using on and off pulsing action, combine until the mixture resembles fine meal.
2. Cut the chilled butter into small pieces, and pulse a few times, or until the mixture resembles coarse meal.
3. Sprinkle with 4 tbsps. of the ice water, and pulse a few times. The mixture should hold together when pinched.
4. Add more water, if necessary. (This can also be done using a pastry blender or two knives.) Scrape the pastry onto a floured board, form it into a ball, and wrap it with plastic wrap. Refrigerate at least 30 minutes,
5. Preheat the oven to 450 degrees F.

6. While the pastry is chilling, peel and core the apples. Divide the raisins and rum into the core holes, and place 1 tsp. of butter in each core hole.
7. Combine the syrup ingredients in a small saucepan, and bring to a boil.
8. Simmer for 3 minutes, and set aside.
9. Divide the pastry into 4 parts. Form one part into a ball, and place it between two sheets of plastic wrap or wax paper. Flatten with your hands into a "pancake." Roll the pastry into a circle large enough to cover the apple.
10. Place an apple in the center, and bring up the sides to encase it. Pinch the top together, holding the dough with a little water. If the folds seem thick, trim them off and seal the seams with water.
11. Repeat with the remaining apples.
12. Place the apples on a baking sheet, and brush them with the syrup.
13. Place them in the oven and bake for 10 minutes.
14. Reduce the heat to 330"F, and brush again with the syrup.
15. Bake an additional 35 minutes, brushing every 10 minutes.
16. Remove from the oven, and allow to cool for 5 minutes. Serve hot or at room temperature.

Williamsburg Shepherd's Pie

Stew Ingredients:

4 tbsps. unsalted butter
2 pounds lean boneless leg of lamb, cut into 1/2-inch cubes
1/2 pound turnips, peeled and diced
1/2 pound carrots, peeled and diced
3 celery stalks. trimmed and sliced
1 medium onion, peeled and diced
1 tsp. fresh thyme leaves
1/2 cup all-purpose flour
2 cups beef stock or water
1/3 cup tomato paste
Salt and freshly ground black pepper to taste

Potato Topping Ingredients:

2 pounds white or red boiling potatoes, peeled and cut into 1-inch cubes
1/4 pound (1 stick) unsalted butter
1 egg
1 egg yolk
1 tsp. salt. or to taste
1/2 tsp. freshly ground white pepper, or to taste.

Directions:

1. To make the stew, melt the butter in a Dutch oven or large saucepan over medium high heat.
2. Add the lamb and brown on all sides, making sure not to crowd the pan. This may have to be done in batches.
3. Remove the lamb from the pan with a slotted spoon, and set aside.

4. Add the turnips, carrots, celery and onion to the pan, and saute for 3 minutes, stirring frequently, or until the onions are translucent. Return the lamb to the pan along with the thyme, and sprinkle the flour over the lamb and vegetables.
5. Cook over low heat for 3 minutes, stirring frequently, to cook the flour.
6. Add the cold stock or water, raise the heat to medium high, and bring to a boil.
7. Stir in the tomato paste, and season with salt and pepper.
8. Cook the lamb mixture covered over low heat for 40 to 55 minutes, or until the lamb is tender.
9. While the lamb is braising, place the potatoes in salted cold water and bring to a boil over high heat. Boil the potatoes until tender, about 15 minutes.
10. Drain, and then mash the potatoes using a potato masher or hand-held electric mixer with the butter, egg, yolk, salt and pepper.
11. Place the mixture in a pastry bag fitted with a large star tip.
12. To serve, preheat an oven broiler.
13. Place the lamb into a large baking dish or individual dishes, and pipe the potatoes into a latticework pattern on the top.
14. Place 6 inches from the broiler element, and brown the potatoes. Serve immediately.

Williamsburg Collops of Salmon

Ingredients:

12 thin slices, salmon (3 oz. each) Salt and freshly ground black pepper to taste3 tbsps. unsalted butter1 cup flour2 tbsps. fennel seeds3 tbsps. vegetable oil1 small head cabbage, tough core removed and thinly shreddedLemon wedges and chopped parsley, for garnish2 tbsps. red wine vinegar

Directions:

1. Working with one slice at a time, place the salmon between 2 pieces of plastic wrap. Use a heavy rolling pin, the back of a knife, or a mallet to pound each 1/2?inch thick.
2. Place the slices on a plate and refrigerate, tightly covered, until ready to serve.
3. In a large skillet over medium heat, melt the butter.
4. Add the fennel seeds and cook, stirring, often, until lightly browned, about 2 minutes.
5. Stir in the cabbage and vinegar, season with salt and pepper, and reduce the heat to low.
6. Cover and cook stirring often, until the cabbage is very tender, about 45 minutes. Check often.
7. Add small amounts of water if necessary to prevent scorching.
8. Season the pounded salmon slices on both sides with salt and pepper.
9. In a large shallow bowl, place the flour and add the salmon, one slice at a time. Turn to coat and shake off the excess flour In a large skillet over high heat, heat the vegetable oil.
10. Add the salmon and cook until golden brown, about 2 minutes on each side.

11. Place the cabbage: on a warmed serving platter and arrange the salmon slices on top, overlapping. Garnish with the lemon wedges and parsley.

Williamsburg Veal Chop

Ingredients:

4 loin veal chops (10 oz. each)
Salt and freshly ground black pepper to taste
2 tbsps. unsalted butter
2 tbsps. vegetable oil
1 cup sliced celery
1 cup sliced mushrooms (leave very small mushrooms whole)
1 tsp. fresh thyme
1/4 cup Port
1/2 cup veal or beef stock

Directions:

1. Season the veal chops with salt and pepper to taste.
2. Heat the butter and oil in a large saute pan or skillet over medium high heat. When hot, add the veal chops, being careful not to crowd the pan, and sear the chops on both sides until brown.
3. Remove the chops from the pan and set aside.
4. Add the celery to the pan, and saute over medium heat for 2 minutes, stirring frequently.
5. Add the mushrooms and thyme to the pan, and saute for 3 additional minutes. Deglaze the pan with the Port and stock.
6. Season with salt and pepper.
7. Return the veal chops to the pan, and braise uncovered, turning once, for a total of 5 to 8 minutes, or until the chops reach desired color.
8. Serve immediately, with the vegetables on top of the chops.

Williamsburg Bourbon Balls

Ingredients:

2 cups vanilla wafer crumbs
2 tbsps. cocoa
1 1/2 cups confectioner's sugar, divided
1 cup pecans, very finely chopped
2 tbsps. white corn syrup
1/4 cup bourbon

Directions:

1. Mix well the vanilla wafer crumbs, cocoa, 1cup confectioner's sugar, and pecans.
2. Add corn syrup and bourbon; mix well.
3. Shape into 1-inch balls and roll in the remaining confectioner's sugar.
4. Put in tightly covered tin box or other metal container for at least 12 hours before serving.

Williamsburg Creamed Celery with Pecans

Ingredients:

4 cups celery, cut diagonally in ½-inch pieces2 tbsps. butter2 tbsps. All-purpose flour2 cups milk1 tsp. salt¾ cup pecan halves buttered bread crumbs

Directions:

1. Preheat the oven to 400 degrees F.
2. Grease a 1 ½-quart casserole.
3. Boil the celery in enough water to cover until tender; drain.
4. Melt the butter over medium heat.
5. Stir in the flour and slowly add the milk to make a cream sauce, stirring until thick and smooth.
6. Add the salt and well-drained celery.
7. Spoon into the prepared casserole, top with pecans, and cover with buttered bread crumbs.
8. Bake at 400 degrees F. for 15 minutes.

Colonial Williamsburg Pumpkin Gnocchi

Ingredients:

3 medium size Idaho potatoes
1 1/2 cup sifted all-purpose flour
1 1/2 cup sifted cake flour
2 eggs
1/2 cup pumpkin puree
1 tsp. salt

Directions:

1. Boil potatoes whole and unpeeled.
2. Combine flours on workbench.
3. Crack eggs into center of flour.
4. When potatoes are cooked throughout, strain, then peel.
5. While still hot, process potatoes through food mill directly into flour and eggs.
6. Add pumpkin puree.
7. Knead softly until everything is combined evenly.
8. Cover dough ball with plastic wrap.
9. Working swiftly while dough is warm, roll dough into small logs in increments of about two centimeters in diameter.
10. Cut log into — inch pieces.
11. Roll pieces into balls.
12. Roll balls into boiling salted water off the back of a fork.
13. When they float, they are done.
14. Strain and add sauce.

Colonial Williamsburg Welsh Rabbit

Ingredients:

1 cup beer
2 tsps. mustard powder
1/4 tsp. cayenne pepper
1 tsp. Worcestershire sauce
1 1/2 cups grated Cheddar cheese
2 tbsps. unsalted butter
Salt to taste
4 to 6 tomato slices
8 to 12 slices (1/2 inch thick), toasted French or Italian bread

Directions:

1. Preheat a broiler.
2. Place the beer, mustard, cayenne and Worcestershire sauce in a saucepan, and heat over medium heat until boiling. Slowly whisk in the cheese, making sure each addition is melted before adding the next.
3. Add the butter, and whisk until smooth.
4. Season with salt to taste, and set aside.
5. Place the tomato slices on the rack of a broiler pan, and broil for 1 minute, or until lightly browned.
6. To serve, place the toast slices on the bottom of an oven-proof gratin dish or in individual gratin dishes.
7. Pour the cheese over the toast, and then top with the tomato slices.
8. Place under the broiler and broil until the cheese is bubbly and brown. Serve immediately.

Colonial Williamsburg Tidewater Chili

Ingredients:

4 large onions, chopped
1 1/2 tbsps. basil
4 cloves garlic, minced
1/3 cup chili powder
1/3 cup peanut oil
2 tbsps. cumin
3 cans (28 oz. each) Italian plum tomatoes
2 pounds smoked sausage
2 cans (29 oz. each) tomato puree
5 pounds lean chuck
2 tbsps. crushed red pepper flakes
4 cans (15 oz. each) red kidney beans, drained
1 tbsp. salt

Directions:

1. Sauté the onion and garlic in the peanut oil over medium heat.
2. Stir in the tomatoes, tomato puree, and herbs and spices and simmer while cooking the meats.
3. Cut the sausage into 1/2-inch pieces and brown.
4. Drain and add to the mixture.
5. Brown the chuck in small batches.
6. Drain and add to the mixture.
7. Simmer for 1 hour.
8. Add the beans.

Colonial Williamsburg Chilled Cream of Asparagus Soup

Ingredients:

2 cups chicken stock* or canned chicken broth 1 15-oz. can asparagus spears, drained1 small onion, chopped 1/2 small bay leaf 3 tbsps. butter 3 tbsps. flour1 cup milk salt and white pepper.
1/4 cup whipping cream

Directions:

1. Bring chicken stock to boil.
2. Add drained asparagus, onion, and bay leaf.
3. Bring to a boil, reduce heat, and simmer, covered, for 30 minutes. Discard bay leaf.
4. Melt butter in a saucepan.
5. Stir in flour and cook over medium heat for 3 minutes, stirring constantly.
6. Do not let the mixture brown.
7. Heat milk and add it to the butter and flour mixture, whisking until the mixture is smooth and thick.
8. Purée the asparagus-chicken stock mixture in food processor or blender.
9. Strain through a sieve into the milk mixture, pressing down hard on the solids with the back of a wooden spoon.
10. Cook over medium heat, whisking constantly, until the mixture is slightly thickened.
11. Add salt and white pepper to taste. Chill thoroughly.
12. Taste for seasoning after the soup is chilled.
13. Stir in cream just before serving.

Williamsburg Chicken Stock

Ingredients:

1/2 tsp. thyme1 bay leaf
1/2 tsp marjoram
3 sprigs parsley
6 peppercorns
2 onions, slice
salt
3 ribs celery with leaves, sliced
3 carrots, sliced
2 leeks, sliced
5 pounds chicken necks, backs, and wings.

Directions:

1. Tie the thyme, bay leaf, marjoram, parsley, and peppercorns in a cheesecloth bag.
2. Place in soup pot.
3. Add onions, celery, carrots, leeks, and chicken.
4. Cover with cold water.
5. Bring to a boil, reduce the heat, and simmer partially covered, for 2 to 3 hours, or until the chicken separates easily from the bones.
6. Remove the chicken.
7. Simmer uncovered until the stock is reduces to 4 quarts.
8. Add salt to taste. Refrigerate.
9. Strain the stock and remove all fat.

Williamsburg Avocados Stuffed with Crabmeat Rémoulade

Ingredients:

12 oz. backfin crabmeat
1 tbsp. lemon juice
Rémoulade sauce (recipe below)
2 large ripe avocados
Lettuce
Tomato wedges
Lemon wedges
Black olives

Directions:

1. Pick over the crabmeat and discard bits of shell or cartilage. Gently toss crabmeat with lemon juice and fold in the Rémoulade Sauce.
2. Peel the avocados, halve them, and remove seeds.
3. Arrange lettuce leaves on each of 4 plates.
4. Place an avocado half on each plate.
5. Fill the center with crabmeat mixture. Garnish with tomato and lemon wedges and black olives.

Rémoulade Sauce

Ingredients:

1 tsp. capers, finely chopped
1 tsp. gherkins, finely chopped
1/2 tsp. fresh tarragon, finely chopped
1 anchovy fillet, finely chopped
3/4 tsp. Dijon mustard
3/4 cup. mayonnaise*

Directions:

1. Combine capers, gherkins, tarragon, and anchovy fillet.
2. Add mustard and mayonnaise.
3. Mix well, and chill thoroughly.

Williamsburg Mayonnaise

Ingredients:

2 egg yolks1/2 tsp Dijon mustard1/2 tsp salt1/8 tsp white pepper1/2 cup vegetable oil1/2 cup olive oil2 tbsps. white wine vinegar, or lemon juice

Directions:

1. Allow all ingredients and bowl to come to room temperature.
2. Whisk egg yolks, mustard, salt, and white pepper together in a small bowl.
3. Add the oils slowly, whisking constantly, until the mayonnaise begins to emulsify.
4. When the mayonnaise has thickened, add the vinegar or lemon juice alternately with the last of the oil.

Colonial Williamsburg Caramel Custard

Ingredients:

2 eggs
2 egg yolks
1/3 cup sugar
2 cups milk
1/8 tsp salt
3/4 tsp vanilla extract
Caramel syrup*

Directions:

1. Preheat the oven to 350 degrees F.
2. Beat eggs and egg yolks.
3. Gradually add sugar and beat until the mixture is light and fluffy.
4. Scald the milk.
5. Gradually pour it over the egg mixture, beating constantly.
6. Add salt and vanilla.
7. Pour into individual custard cups or ovenproof glass dishes.
8. Place dishes in a roasting pan.
9. Fill pan with enough hot water to come 2/3 way up the sides of the dishes.
10. Bake at 350° F. for 30 minutes or until the custard tests done.
11. Remove custard cups from water bath and cool on a rack.
12. Just before serving, run a knife around the edge of the custard and invert into sherbet or champagne glasses.
13. Pour cold caramel syrup over the custards.

Colonial Williamsburg Caramel Syrup

Ingredients:

1/2 cup sugar
1/4 cup cold water
1/2 cup boiling water

Directions:

1. Combine sugar and cold water in heavy saucepan. Swirl mixture until sugar dissolves.
2. Do not stir.
3. Add the boiling water.
4. Boil over medium heat without stirring until the syrup is the color of butterscotch.
5. Remove from heat. Cool. Refrigerate.

Note: the syrup will thicken as it cools.

About the Author

Laura Sommers is **The Recipe Lady!**

She lives on a small farm in Baltimore County, Maryland and has a passion for all things domestic especially when it comes to saving money. She has a profitable eBay business and is a couponing addict. Follow her tips and tricks to learn how to make delicious meals on a budget, save money or to learn the latest life hack!

Follow her on Pinterest:

http://pinterest.com/therecipelady1

Visit the Recipe Lady's blog for even more great recipes:

http://the-recipe-lady.blogspot.com/

Visit her Amazon Author Page to see her latest books:

amazon.com/author/laurasommers

Follow the Recipe Lady on Facebook:

https://www.facebook.com/therecipegirl

Follow her on Twitter:

https://twitter.com/TheRecipeLady1

Other Books by Laura Sommers

- Recipes for Chicken Wings
- 50 Super Awesome Salsa Recipes!
- Delicious Chip Dip Cookbook
- Authentic Traditional Memphis, Tennessee Recipes
- 50 Super Awesome Coleslaw and Potato Salad Recipes

Made in the USA
Middletown, DE
13 January 2023